Rosa Parks?

WITHDRAWN

Who Was Rosa Parks?

By Yona Zeldis McDonough

Illustrated by Stephen Marchesi

Grosset & Dunlap
An Imprint of Penguin Group (USA) Inc.

For my mother, Malcah Zeldis—YZM
For Ketty and Alex, with hope for the future—SM

GROSSET & DUNLAP
Published by the Penguin Group
Penguin Group (USA) Inc., 375 Hudson Street, New York, New York 10014, USA
Penguin Group (Canada), 90 Eglinton Avenue East, Suite 700,
Toronto, Ontario M4P 2Y3, Canada (a division of Pearson Penguin Canada Inc.)
Penguin Books Ltd., 80 Strand, London WC2R 0RL, England
Penguin Group Ireland, 25 St. Stephen's Green, Dublin 2, Ireland
(a division of Penguin Books Ltd.)
Penguin Group (Australia), 250 Camberwell Road, Camberwell, Victoria 3124, Australia
(a division of Pearson Australia Group Pty. Ltd.)
Penguin Books India Pvt. Ltd., 11 Community Centre,
Panchsheel Park, New Delhi—110 017, India
Penguin Group (NZ), 67 Apollo Drive, Rosedale, North Shore 0632, New Zealand
(a division of Pearson New Zealand Ltd.)
Penguin Books (South Africa) (Pty.) Ltd., 24 Sturdee Avenue,
Rosebank, Johannesburg 2196, South Africa

Penguin Books Ltd., Registered Offices:
80 Strand, London WC2R 0RL, England

Text copyright © 2010 by Yona Zeldis McDonough. Interior illustrations copyright ©
2010 by Stephen Marchesi. Cover illustration copyright © 2010 by Nancy Harrison.
All rights reserved. Published by Grosset & Dunlap, a division of
Penguin Young Readers Group, 345 Hudson Street, New York, New York 10014.
GROSSET & DUNLAP is a trademark of Penguin Group (USA) Inc.
Printed in the U.S.A.

Library of Congress Control Number: 2009051593

ISBN 978-0-448-45442-9   10 9 8 7 6 5 4 3 2 1

Contents

Who Was
Rosa Parks?

Every morning, Rosa Parks walked to school. Every afternoon, she walked back home again. There was no school bus to her school. She didn't mind the walk. She was used to it.

Often she saw a big, yellow school bus roll past

her. But the bus never stopped for her. All the children inside were white. It was taking them to a school that was for white students only. Rosa was black.

Rosa grew up in Pine Level, Alabama. At that time in the South, black people and white people led separate lives. All of Rosa's friends and family were black. She hardly knew any white people. How could she? Black people weren't allowed in the same restaurants or hotels. They couldn't swim in public pools with white people or drink from the same water fountains.

Every time she saw a bus carrying white children to and from school, it made her feel like black children didn't matter as much as white children. Sometimes the white children threw trash out the windows, trying to hit the black children. After a while, Rosa and the other black children stopped walking by the road. They went through the fields instead.

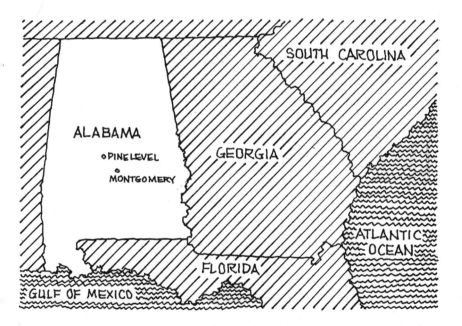

The school for the white children was nicer, too. It had real glass panes in the windows. At Rosa's school, there was no glass, only shutters. Still, Rosa knew inside that she was as good as any white child. She was as good as anyone, and one day she would prove it.

Chapter 1
Down on the Farm

Rosa Louise McCauley was born in Tuskegee, Alabama, on February 4, 1913. Her father, James, was a carpenter. Her mother, Leona, was a teacher. Rosa was small for her age. She was often sick with a sore throat. She had to spend a lot of time in bed.

When Rosa was about two and a half, her mother and father separated. Rosa moved to Pine Level, just outside Montgomery, Alabama. There, she lived on her grandparents' farm with her mother and her little brother, Sylvester. She liked the farm. With her family around, she felt safe and secure.

Beyond the farm, the world was not such a safe place. Some white people living nearby belonged to a group called the Ku Klux Klan. They wore white robes and hoods to cover their faces. Many times, Klan members set fire to houses where black people lived or churches where they prayed. The police did nothing to stop the attacks.

KU KLUX KLAN

THE KU KLUX KLAN, OR KKK AS IT IS KNOWN, IS A HATE GROUP THAT USES THREATS AND VIOLENCE AGAINST BLACKS AND OTHER MINORITIES. THE NAME PROBABLY CAME FROM THE GREEK WORD *KUKLOS*, MEANING "CIRCLE." THE KU KLUX KLAN WAS A CIRCLE, OR BAND, OF BROTHERS. TENNESSEE VETERANS OF THE CONFEDERATE ARMY FOUNDED THE KLAN AFTER THE CIVIL WAR ENDED IN 1865. GROUPS SOON SPREAD THROUGHOUT THE SOUTH. KLAN MEMBERS WORE WHITE ROBES AND POINTED HATS WITH MASKS TO HIDE THEIR FACES. OFTEN THEY LEFT BURNING CROSSES IN FRONT OF THE VICTIMS' HOMES. DURING THE 1920S, WHEN ROSA WAS A CHILD, THE KLAN SPREAD THROUGHOUT THE COUNTRY. AT ONE POINT, THERE WERE ABOUT FOUR MILLION MEMBERS IN THE UNITED STATES. TODAY, THAT NUMBER IS ABOUT FIVE THOUSAND.

When Klan members marched by Rosa's
house, her grandfather stood at the door. He held
a shotgun in his hand. Some nights, he slept in a
rocking chair, the shotgun in his lap. Rosa often
stayed curled up beside him.

Even whites who didn't belong to the Ku Klux Klan could be cruel. A wealthy planter named Moses Hudson would hire black children to pick and chop cotton. He paid them fifty cents a day. The children usually didn't wear shoes, and the hot ground burned their bare feet so badly that they would pick the cotton on their knees. If any blood got on the white cotton, they would be whipped.

JIM CROW LAWS

IN THE SOUTHERN UNITED STATES FROM 1876 TO 1965, JIM CROW LAWS KEPT SEGREGATION—SEPARATION OF BLACKS AND WHITES—IN PUBLIC FACILITIES. BLACKS COULD NOT BUY HOUSES IN WHITE NEIGHBORHOODS OR EAT AT THE SAME RESTAURANTS AS WHITE PEOPLE. THEY EVEN HAD TO BRING THEIR CLOTHES TO ALL-BLACK LAUNDROMATS. THE TERM "JIM CROW" PROBABLY COMES FROM MINSTREL SHOWS OF THE LATE 1800S. WHITE MEN WOULD WEAR BLACK FACE MAKEUP AND MAKE FUN OF AFRICAN AMERICANS. JIM CROW WAS THE NAME OF A CHARACTER IN MINSTREL SHOW SKITS.

Even so, Rosa did not mistrust all white people.
There was an old white woman in Pine Level who
used to take her bass fishing. This woman was
kind and polite to Rosa and her grandparents. She
treated them as equals. There was a white soldier
who always patted her on the head whenever he
came through town. Even a small gesture like this

was unusual. As she grew older, Rosa began to pity the whites who called her names or threw rocks at her. She wanted to forgive, not hate, people who insulted her.

Much of the time, Rosa was happy in Pine Level. She loved school. She couldn't wait for each day to begin. She enjoyed Mother Goose

nursery rhymes, playing hide-and-seek with her friends, and looking after her younger brother. She liked to explore the woods, creeks, and ponds near the farm. (But she was always careful to avoid poisonous snakes!) For extra pocket money, she sold eggs to the neighbors.

Sometimes she wandered into the local cemetery. Some of the tombstones dated back to the Civil War. At the end of the Civil War in 1865, slavery ended. From then on, it was against the law for a person to own another person. Some of Rosa's grandparents had been slaves. Now, even though they were poor and often mistreated, Rosa's family was free.

BROWN VS. BOARD OF EDUCATION

AS A BLACK CHILD LIVING IN THE SOUTH, ROSA PARKS COULD NOT ATTEND SCHOOL WITH WHITE CHILDREN. THEN, IN 1954, A GROUP OF BLACK PARENTS IN TOPEKA, KANSAS, WENT TO COURT TO END SCHOOL SEGREGATION. THEIR CASE IS ONE OF THE MOST FAMOUS EVER TO COME BEFORE THE SUPREME COURT.

THE BLACK PARENTS WERE UPSET BECAUSE THE ALL-BLACK SCHOOL WAS OVER A MILE AWAY FROM THEIR NEIGHBORHOOD. IT WAS A LONG TRIP FOR YOUNG CHILDREN. THE ALL-WHITE ELEMENTARY SCHOOL WAS VERY CLOSE BY. IT WAS UNFAIR THAT THEIR CHILDREN COULD NOT GO THERE.

UP TO THIS POINT, THE LAW SAID PUBLIC SCHOOLS COULD STAY SEGREGATED AS LONG AS THE BLACK SCHOOLS WERE AS GOOD AS THE WHITE SCHOOLS. BUT NOW, THE JUDGES ON THE SUPREME COURT CHANGED THE LAW. FROM HERE ON IN, SEPARATE SCHOOLS FOR BLACK CHILDREN AND WHITE CHILDREN WERE ILLEGAL. PUBLIC SCHOOLS HAD TO BE INTEGRATED. BLACK CHILDREN COULD GO TO ANY PUBLIC SCHOOL THEY WISHED.

Chapter 2
City Lights

In 1924, when Rosa was eleven, her mother sent her to live with relatives in Montgomery, the Alabama state capital, so she could go to a better school. It was called the Montgomery Industrial School for Girls. The school had been started by white northerners to help poor black girls. There were

ALICE WHITE

two hundred and fifty to three hundred students. All the teachers were white women from the North. The head of the school, Alice White, was both strict and loving. She expected a lot from her girls. Rosa adored her. From Miss White, Rosa learned to respect herself. She would not set low goals for herself just because she was black.

Rosa was excited to be in Montgomery. To her, it seemed like a big, modern city. Early cars—Model Ts—crowded the streets. There were fine shops filled with fancy dresses, hats, and gloves. A football stadium seated twelve thousand people. Trains on the Louisville & Nashville Railroad lines came charging into Union Station, and riverboats brought their cargo of pine and cotton to the wharf.

But in some ways, Montgomery was just like Pine Level. One day, Rosa was walking through a white neighborhood. A white boy on roller skates sped by and slammed into her. He was trying to shove her off the sidewalk. She turned and pushed him back. The boy's mother was standing nearby. She told Rosa that she could be put in jail

for what she had done—forever. In *Rosa Parks: My Story*, Rosa later wrote, "So I told her that he had pushed me and that I didn't want to be pushed, seeing that I wasn't bothering him at all." She wanted to stand up for herself—and she did.

Rosa spent four years at Miss White's school. Many whites in Montgomery resented Miss White and the other teachers. What business did they have teaching black children? Why didn't they just stay up north where they were from? Twice, the school was set on fire. In 1928, it was forced to close. Miss White went back home to Massachusetts. However, she stayed in touch with Rosa, who considered her a loving teacher and dear friend.

After that, Rosa attended another all-black school. She was hoping to become a teacher, like her mother. Then her grandmother got sick. Rosa, who was sixteen, dropped out of school and moved back to Pine Level to help care for her.

After her grandmother died, Rosa's mother
became ill. Again, Rosa was there to help. She
was not happy about leaving school. But she did
not complain. To make money, she cleaned

houses for white people. Sometimes that wasn't
enough. So she'd stand on the street selling fruit.

Rosa worked hard.

She also belonged to the St. Paul AME Church.
AME stands for African Methodist Episcopal.
The church was in the oldest black neighborhood
in Montgomery. It was the center of Rosa's life
and brought her great joy. Her strong faith helped
her to get through her long, tiring days.

THE ROLE OF THE BLACK CHURCH

THE FIRST BLACK CHURCHES WERE FORMED BEFORE 1800 BY FREE BLACKS IN PHILADELPHIA, PENNSYLVANIA; PETERSBURG, VIRGINIA; AND SAVANNAH, GEORGIA. THE CHURCHES BEGAN BECAUSE BLACKS WERE NOT WELCOME AT MANY WHITE CHURCHES. IN THEIR OWN CHURCHES, BLACKS DEVELOPED A BRAND OF CHRISTIANITY THAT DREW ON AFRICAN SPIRITUAL CUSTOMS.

THE CHURCHES BECAME CENTERS OF THEIR
COMMUNITIES. THE CHURCHES FOUNDED SCHOOLS
AND HELPED THE POOR AND THOSE IN PRISON.
IN THE 1960S, THE CHURCHES WERE A VERY
IMPORTANT PART OF THE CIVIL RIGHTS MOVEMENT.
THEIR MINISTERS BECAME CIVIL RIGHTS LEADERS.
MARTIN LUTHER KING, JR., WAS A MINISTER; SO
WAS JESSE JACKSON.

The church taught her not to complain or rebel. Instead, she was to place her faith in God. God would take care of her. God would provide. But then she met a bright young man named Raymond Parks. Raymond had a lot of different ideas.

Chapter 3
Life with Raymond

Rosa was eighteen when she met Raymond. He was twenty-eight and working at a barbershop in Montgomery. A friend introduced them. Rosa was impressed by how smart he was. Raymond hadn't had much schooling. But he loved learning.

Raymond had suffered through hard times, too. Like Rosa's father, Raymond's father had been a carpenter. He had died falling from a roof when Raymond was a little boy.

His mother, who had taught him to read and write, died when he was a teenager. Since then, Raymond had been on his own. Raymond talked a lot about the lives of blacks in the South. He was one of the first members of the Montgomery chapter of the National Association for the Advancement of Colored People (NAACP). People liked and respected him.

When Raymond and Rosa met, he was upset about a trial in Scottsboro, Alabama.

Nine black teenagers were accused of attacking two white women on a train. The evidence against the boys was faked. The women were lying. Still, the jury convicted eight of the nine boys. They were all sentenced to death except for the youngest. He was only twelve. (Later, most of the sentences were lifted. However, the eight boys served at least six years in prison for a crime they hadn't committed.)

Raymond Parks could not stop thinking and

talking about this case. In fact, he could have been killed for his efforts to bring attention to the Scottsboro boys. Rosa was moved by Raymond's courage. And she was proud of him.

On their first date, Raymond took Rosa for a ride in his shiny, red sports car. On their second date, he proposed. Two years later, in December 1932, they were married in Pine Level. The couple moved to Montgomery, not far from Alabama State University.

NATIONAL ASSOCIATION FOR THE ADVANCEMENT OF COLORED PEOPLE (NAACP)

FOUNDED FEBRUARY 12, 1909, THE NAACP IS AMERICA'S OLDEST, LARGEST, AND MOST FAMOUS CIVIL RIGHTS GROUP. AMONG ITS FOUNDING MEMBERS WAS THE FAMOUS WRITER AND HISTORIAN, W.E.B. DU BOIS. THE NAACP BEGAN, IN PART, TO STOP LYNCHINGS (WHEN AN ANGRY GROUP OF PEOPLE SEIZES AND HANGS SOMEONE WITHOUT A TRIAL). THE GOAL OF THE NAACP HAS BEEN TO END RACIAL HATRED AND HELP MINORITIES WHO ARE DENIED THEIR CIVIL RIGHTS. THE NAACP CELEBRATED ITS ONE HUNDREDTH ANNIVERSARY IN 2009.

W.E.B. DU BOIS

Raymond continued his work for the Scottsboro boys. He held meetings in the Parks' front room. Rosa never forgot the first meeting. The men brought guns. They felt they needed to protect themselves; what they were doing was dangerous.

Rosa sat on the back porch, her face buried in her lap. It made Rosa sad that black men feared for their lives just because they were holding a meeting! Still, her husband's work spurred her on. Raymond wanted Rosa to go back to school. And she did.

In 1934, she earned her high school diploma. At that time, hardly any black people in Montgomery were high school graduates. Not

even one in ten. Rosa was proud to be among the small number of blacks who did have a degree. Yet she was still unable to find work that really challenged her. Instead, she took a job at a hospital as a nurse's assistant. She also did sewing on the side.

Then, in 1941, she got a job as a secretary at an army air force base in Montgomery called Maxwell Field. President Franklin D. Roosevelt

had forbidden segregation at all United States
military bases. So Maxwell Field was integrated.
Blacks and whites worked together. But when Rosa
left the base, she had to ride home on a segregated
bus. Blacks had to sit in the back. It was unfair
and it made her deeply angry. Rosa Parks was a
quiet person. But the anger lived inside her,
growing day by day. Soon it became so large, she
knew she would have to do something about it.

Chapter 4
The Call to Action

Raymond was growing frustrated with the NAACP. He dropped out in 1943. He thought that the educated men in charge did not understand the needs of working-class black men like him.

But that same year, Rosa decided to join the NAACP. She went to her first meeting hoping to

see Johnnie Mae Carr, an old friend from Miss White's school. Johnnie Mae was not there that evening. Rosa stayed anyway. Because she was the only woman in the room, she was asked to take notes.

For the next twelve years, Rosa served as the secretary for the NAACP in Montgomery. She was one of the few women in the civil rights movement during the 1940s. Her boss was a man named Edgar Daniel Nixon. Nixon worked as a porter on a train. He had traveled all over the country. He saw how different life was for black people in the North. Nixon wanted that kind of integration in the South, too. That was his dream. He believed strongly in the rights of black people.

E.D. NIXON

But did he care about women's rights? No. Nixon believed that women should stay in one place— the kitchen. Rosa's quick answer, "What about me?" made him laugh.

Rosa was an excellent secretary. She typed notes, wrote letters, and organized meetings. Rosa let people know about hateful crimes against black people—beatings and lynchings. She helped find lawyers for black people accused of crimes they didn't commit. Rosa also helped black people register to vote. (Registering means getting your name on a list of voters in your district so, on election day, you can vote.)

Voting is one of the most basic rights in a democracy. Voting is the way to show who you want in office and what laws you want passed. Yet of the fifty thousand black people living in Montgomery, only thirty-one were registered to vote. And some of those people were dead! So Rosa decided to change things starting with herself. She was going to register to vote.

It was not easy to do. The registration office was only open during certain hours. These were hours when most people worked. Next, she had to take a reading test. This test was only given to

black people, not whites. And it was not really about reading. It was a long, hard test about rules of government. Most people would not be able to answer the questions. Rosa took the test three times before she passed. The day her registration came in the mail, she was very excited. But she still could not vote yet.

She had to pay a poll tax. According to Alabama law, at age twenty-one, voters had to start paying a tax of $1.50 per year to vote. Rosa was now thirty-two. That meant she owed eleven years of poll taxes, or $16.50. That doesn't sound

like a lot of money. But in 1945, a movie ticket might cost ten cents and an ice cream cone five. Sixteen dollars and fifty cents was a lot of money. Still, Rosa paid it. When election day came, she cast her vote for Alabama's governor. Rosa was thrilled. But she was angry, too. Getting the right to vote had been long, hard, and expensive. Many black people would not be able to get past all the hurdles. She knew that voting was a way black people could improve their lives. "With the vote . . ." she declared, ". . . we would have a voice."

In order for that voice to be heard, it needed to become louder. It was not enough that Rosa could vote. Other blacks living in the South needed to vote.

Rosa Parks was determined to help them become registered voters.

Chapter 5
Back of the Bus

World War II ended in 1945. American soldiers returned home. Rosa's brother, Sylvester, was among them. He had been in an army medical unit. He carried wounded soldiers on stretchers off battlefields. Sylvester had been in Europe and the South Pacific. In

SYLVESTER McCAULEY

Europe, black soldiers were seen as heroes, just like white soldiers. But once back in the United States, black soldiers faced the same prejudices as before the war.

Sylvester returned to Alabama but found it too hard now to take the insults and threats of white racists. He and his family moved north to Detroit, Michigan. He begged Rosa and Raymond to join him there.

Rosa visited Detroit. Yes, it was amazing to see blacks sitting next to whites on public buses. But in many other ways Detroit was not much

different from Montgomery. In 1943, race riots in Detroit had killed thirty-four people and wounded hundreds more, black and white. Rosa and Raymond decided against moving north.

Life did not get any easier for Rosa. Raymond's health was bad so he could not earn much. Rosa's mother was living with them now, too. Rosa cleaned houses for white people. She also did sewing at a tailor's shop and later on at a department store.

Still, Rosa continued to work for free for the NAACP. She became an adviser to its youth group.

Although she and Raymond never had any of their own, Rosa loved children. She felt a special bond with them. She urged young black people to integrate the main public library in Montgomery. But every time the black students tried to check out books, they were refused.

The public buses were still very much on Rosa's mind. The rules for riding the bus were complicated. There were thirty-six seats on each bus. The front rows were for white passengers. The back rows were for blacks. The middle rows

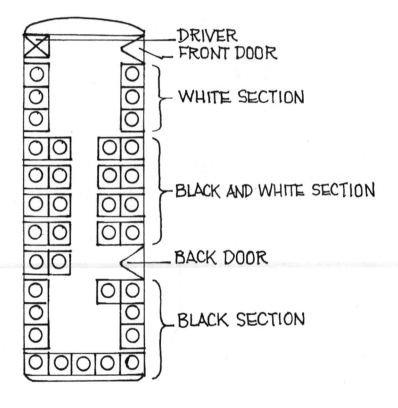

DRIVER
FRONT DOOR
WHITE SECTION
BLACK AND WHITE SECTION
BACK DOOR
BLACK SECTION

were for whites and blacks. But black people could not sit in the same row with white people. So if a white person sat down in a row, all the blacks in that row had to get up and move. Even if the back of the bus was full and the front was empty, black people could not sit there. They had to stand in the back.

Rosa felt ashamed every single time she climbed aboard one of those buses. And yet, she had to ride the bus to get to work. So did many other black people. A bus seat may seem like a little thing. But it wasn't. It represented something big. One afternoon, Rosa paid her fare and got on the Cleveland Avenue bus. The bus was very crowded. In the rear, black people stood tightly pressed together. Some had to stand in the back stairs. So Rosa got on the bus through the front door. She was moving back when the driver ordered Rosa to get off the bus. He wanted her to get back on again through the rear door.

Rosa refused. Why should she get off the bus just to get on again? The driver told her that she had better obey him. Still, Rosa did not move.

The driver stopped the bus. He grabbed her by her coat and began yanking her along. Before she reached the front door, she sat down in an empty seat . . . a seat for white people.

"Get off my bus!" the driver shouted.

Finally Rosa did. But she had made her point.

Chapter 6
A Visit to Highlander

In 1954, Rosa made an important new friend: Virginia Durr. Virginia was a white woman born and raised in Birmingham, Alabama. Growing up, she had been taught that white people were better than black people. However, she went to college in Massachusetts. At Wellesley College,

Virginia's ideas began to change. She took classes with black students; she had meals at the same table as black students. Later, she married a lawyer named Clifford Durr, who believed in equality for black people. They eventually settled in Montgomery, where Clifford opened a law practice. Most of his clients were black. Virginia worked with black women's groups. She was also part of a prayer group. It was in this prayer group

VIRGINIA AND CLIFFORD DURR

that Virginia and Rosa became friends. The new friends had much to say to each other. Virginia and Rosa talked endlessly about how to end racism. Virginia described Rosa as quiet but brave.

She noticed that people had great respect for Rosa, and that when Rosa felt at ease among people, she had a good sense of humor. As close as the two women became, Rosa would never call Virginia by her first name. For twenty years, they addressed each other as Mrs. Parks and Mrs. Durr.

Virginia helped Rosa attend a ten-day training workshop at a school called Highlander in Monteagle, Tennessee. It taught people to fight for workers' rights and equal rights for blacks. The students came from the north, south, east, and west. They were black and white, young and old.

Many famous people, including Reverend Martin Luther King, Jr., attended the school.

Rosa was excited about going to Tennessee for the workshop. In July 1955, she took a leave of absence from her tailoring job. One of Virginia Durr's daughters loaned her a suitcase, and off she went.

The workshop was an eye-opener for Rosa. She was forty-two years old. For the first time in her life, she was living among people for whom color didn't seem to matter. People forgot what color a person was. White people treated blacks with dignity and respect. Chores were divided up fairly. Rosa was not asked to wait on white people; she worked as an equal beside them. Rosa attended classes on voting rights and desegregation.

She was nervous at first. But everybody was so warm and friendly, she soon relaxed. She shared what it was like to be black and poor in the South. She even joined in the sing-alongs. One of the most famous civil rights songs, "We Shall Overcome," first became popular at this school.

When the workshop in Tennessee ended, everyone was given an assignment. They had to figure out what might make things change in their own small towns. Rosa didn't see how anything was going to change in Montgomery, Alabama. However, her time in Tennessee had changed Rosa. She went home feeling uplifted and stronger. She wanted to keep on working for equality.

"WE SHALL OVERCOME"

THE REVEREND CHARLES TINDLEY WROTE THE GOSPEL SONG "WE SHALL OVERCOME" AROUND 1900. ZILPHIA HORTON, MUSIC DIRECTOR OF THE SCHOOL IN TENNESSEE THAT ROSA ATTENDED, DISCOVERED IT MANY YEARS LATER. SHE TAUGHT THE SONG TO OTHERS. NEW WORDS AND VERSES WERE ADDED OVER TIME. THE SONG IS SIMPLE AND POWERFUL. AT MARCHES, BLACKS AND WHITES HELD HANDS AND SANG IT TOGETHER. "WE SHALL OVERCOME" BECAME THE THEME SONG OF THE CIVIL RIGHTS MOVEMENT. HERE ARE SOME OF ITS MOST FAMOUS WORDS:

WE SHALL OVERCOME
WE SHALL OVERCOME
WE SHALL OVERCOME SOME DAY
OH, DEEP IN MY HEART
I DO BELIEVE
WE SHALL OVERCOME SOME DAY

Chapter 7
A New Day

It bothered Rosa even more now to ride on the segregated buses in Montgomery. It wasn't right for black people to be treated this way. Often she walked rather than ride a bus. Things were not much better at her job at the department store.

She had to smile and act politely even when people were rude to her. She continued her work with the NAACP. She met Dr. Martin Luther King, Jr. He was the new minister at the most important black church in town, Dexter Avenue Baptist.

MARTIN LUTHER KING, JR.

She also met Adam Clayton Powell, Jr., a black congressman from New York City. Rosa hoped both of these men could help the blacks of Montgomery.

ADAM CLAYTON POWELL, JR.

MARTIN LUTHER KING, JR.

DR. MARTIN LUTHER KING, JR., BELIEVED IN NONVIOLENT PROTEST. FOR INSTANCE, IN THE MID-1960S, HE ORGANIZED SIT-INS AT LUNCH COUNTERS IN THE SOUTH THAT WOULD NOT SERVE BLACK PEOPLE. GROUPS OF BLACK STUDENTS WOULD SIT AT A LUNCH COUNTER AND ASK TO BE SERVED. ALTHOUGH THE ANSWER WAS ALWAYS NO, THE STUDENTS REFUSED TO GET UP AND LEAVE. OFTEN THEY WERE ARRESTED AND TREATED HARSHLY BY POLICE. BUT THEY NEVER FOUGHT BACK. THEY WERE ALWAYS POLITE. EVENTUALLY, THE SIT-INS BEGAN TO GET NATIONAL ATTENTION.

KING WAS ARRESTED THIRTY TIMES FOR THIS KIND OF CIVIL DISOBEDIENCE. HIS WORDS AND DEEDS INSPIRED BLACK PEOPLE TO JOIN THE CIVIL RIGHTS MOVEMENT. IN APRIL 1968, KING WAS SHOT TO DEATH IN MEMPHIS, TENNESSEE.

On Tuesday, December 1, 1955, Rosa left work a little before five o'clock. She walked down to Court Square to catch the Cleveland Avenue bus. She got on and paid her fare. Only then did she realize who the driver was. It was the same driver who had tried to drag her off the bus

twelve years before. His name was Jim Blake. Rosa said nothing and sat down in one of the seats reserved for blacks. Soon the bus filled up. There were no more seats in the white section.

In *Rosa Parks: My Story*, Rosa described what happened after that. A white man had to stand. Blake called out to Rosa and the other black people sitting in that row. "Move y'all. I want those two seats." At first, no one stirred or spoke. Blake's voice got louder. "Y'all better make it light on yourselves and let me have those seats!"

Two men and a woman in Rosa's row got up. Rosa let them pass. But she did not get up. Instead, she slid over to the window. Later on, she said that she stayed seated because: "The more we gave in and complied, the worse they treated us."

The driver marched over to Rosa. "Are you going to stand up?" he snarled.

"No." Rosa's voice was quiet but firm.

"Well, I'm going to have you arrested," he said.

"You may do that," Rosa replied.

Everyone on the bus was silent. Rosa thought of her grandfather and his shotgun. She thought about all the insults over so many years. She felt as if she had "the strength of [her] ancestors with [her]." She made her choice. And she was sticking by it.

The driver went to call the police. The police car pulled up a few minutes later. The officers took Rosa off the bus. They didn't handcuff her. And they did not hurt her. To Rosa, they seemed tired; they didn't want to deal with a minor crime. But they still took Rosa to the police desk

at city hall. She was booked and fingerprinted.
When she asked to drink from the water fountain,
she was told that it was for whites only. She would
have to wait until she got to jail.

Jail!

All Rosa had wanted was to stay in her seat.
Now she was in jail. She was led down a long,

dark hall and put in a cell. She was allowed to make one phone call, so Rosa called her mother. Her mother was very worried. She wanted to know if Rosa had been beaten. Rosa said no.

Raymond Parks borrowed a car and went to get Rosa. By this time, other people knew about Rosa's arrest. Rosa's bail was set at one hundred dollars. Rosa and Raymond did not have that much money. Neither did Virginia and Clifford Durr. Luckily, Edgar Nixon from the NAACP was able to pay the bail. Rosa was released.

The first person Rosa saw was Virginia Durr. Virginia was just happy to see that at least Rosa wasn't in handcuffs. The two friends hugged tightly.

Rosa went home. She was totally worn out. She was going to be put on trial! Yet right away Nixon asked her to think past the trial. He wanted Rosa to consider bringing a lawsuit against the city bus company. People sue other people or businesses when they feel something unfair has been done to them.

Rosa's lawsuit would ask judges to state that the seating rules in public buses were against the law. If the judges did that, then people, black or white, could sit wherever they wanted.

At first, Raymond did not want her to do it. He was afraid she might be hurt or even killed. Rosa understood his fear. At the very least she would lose her job. She might even be arrested again. And how would a trial affect her mother, who was old and sick?

Rosa thought it over. Then she said yes. She would bring a lawsuit. Jim Crow laws had to end. She wanted to help do that. Black people deserved the same freedom that white people enjoyed. Nixon was thrilled. Rosa was the right person to bring the lawsuit. She was hardworking. She had no police record. In *Rosa Parks: My Story*, she said, "White people couldn't point to me and say there was anything I had done to deserve such treatment except be born black."

NELSON MANDELA

IN 1990, ROSA PARKS MET NELSON MANDELA, THE GREAT BLACK LEADER FROM SOUTH AFRICA WHO HAD BROUGHT AN END TO THE EVIL SYSTEM OF APARTHEID IN HIS HOMELAND.

BORN IN SOUTH AFRICA IN 1918, NELSON MANDELA WAS THE SON OF A TEMBU CHIEF. HE BECAME A LAWYER AND TRIED TO CHALLENGE THE LAWS OF APARTHEID. APARTHEID WAS A SYSTEM OF LAWS AGAINST BLACK PEOPLE IN SOUTH AFRICA. THESE LAWS ALLOWED THE WHITES IN POWER TO LEGALLY MURDER, ENSLAVE, IMPRISON, AND PERSECUTE BLACK PEOPLE. APARTHEID ALSO MEANT WHITES AND BLACKS HAD TO LIVE, WORK, AND TRAVEL SEPARATELY. IT WAS AN EVIL SYSTEM THAT REMAINED IN PLACE FOR DECADES UNTIL BRAVE MEN LIKE MANDELA HELPED END IT. HE WAS PUT IN JAIL, WHERE HE REMAINED FOR TWENTY-SEVEN YEARS. DURING THIS TIME, HIS REPUTATION GREW. EVEN BEHIND BARS, HE BECAME THE MOST IMPORTANT BLACK LEADER IN SOUTH AFRICA AND A SYMBOL OF RESISTANCE. HE WAS RELEASED ON FEBRUARY 11, 1990. AFTER HIS RELEASE, HE CONTINUED HIS WORK, AND WAS ELECTED SOUTH AFRICA'S FIRST BLACK PRESIDENT. HE WON THE NOBEL PEACE PRIZE IN 1993.

Fred Gray was one of
two black lawyers in
Montgomery. He agreed
to take on Rosa's case
for free. But Rosa
needed more than a
good lawyer. She
needed the entire black
community behind her.
All the black people in
Montgomery, not just

FRED GRAY

Rosa Parks, had to rise up against the bus
companies.

Chapter 8
"No Riders Today!"

There are many ways to protest. Sometimes people march and carry signs for their cause. Sometimes they boycott a company. That means refusing to do business with that company.

Rosa's lawyer wanted all the black people in Montgomery to boycott—he wanted them to

avoid riding the public buses for a single day. That might make the bus companies realize how much they needed black passengers. Without them, the bus companies would lose a lot of money. If they wanted black riders to return, they would have to treat them better.

The boycott was set for Monday, December 5, 1955. Nixon and the others chose that date because it was the day of Rosa's trial.

Thousands of handbills were run by students and professors at Alabama State College, telling people about the boycott. Posters saying "Remember we are fighting for a cause" were hung up across the city.

Remember We are
Fighting For a cause
Do Not- Ride A
Bus Today

CLAUDETTE COLVIN

NINE MONTHS BEFORE ROSA PARKS WAS ARRESTED, A HIGH SCHOOL STUDENT NAMED CLAUDETTE COLVIN REFUSED TO GIVE UP HER SEAT ON A MONTGOMERY CITY BUS. HER FAMILY DIDN'T OWN A CAR, SO SHE RELIED ON CITY BUSES TO GET TO SCHOOL. ON MARCH 2, 1955, A DRIVER ORDERED HER AND THREE OTHER BLACK PASSENGERS TO GIVE UP THEIR SEATS TO FOUR WHITE PASSENGERS. CLAUDETTE COLVIN REFUSED. POLICE OFFICERS WERE CALLED. ONE OF THEM KICKED HER AND KNOCKED THE BOOKS FROM HER ARMS. CRYING, SHE WAS HANDCUFFED AND TAKEN TO JAIL BEFORE BEING SET FREE. EVEN THOUGH SHE HAD BEEN TREATED TERRIBLY, EDGAR NIXON DID NOT THINK CLAUDETTE WAS THE BEST PERSON TO CHALLENGE BUS SEGREGATION. CLAUDETTE WAS ONLY FIFTEEN AND PREGNANT. THE POLICE ACCUSED HER OF CURSING. (CLAUDETTE DENIED THIS.) ROSA PARKS SEEMED LIKE A BETTER CIVIL RIGHTS "ROLE MODEL" TO THE NAACP. CLAUDETTE COLVIN WAS EVERY BIT AS BRAVE AS ROSA BUT HER NAME IS OFTEN LEFT OUT OF THE STORY OF THE CIVIL RIGHTS MOVEMENT.

On Friday, the handbills were given out on the street and in schools, businesses, barbershops, and beauty salons. They were given out in factories, too. By Friday afternoon, nearly every black person in Montgomery had a flyer. Edgar Nixon helped with the boycott. He called the city's black ministers. On Sunday, many of the black ministers in town urged churchgoers to support the boycott.

Now the question was: On Monday, would black people ride the buses or not?

On Monday morning, Rosa was nervous. She peered out her window. An empty bus rolled down Cleveland Avenue. Across town, on South Jackson Street, two empty buses went by.

Soon the streets were packed with black people walking to schools, factories, or downtown to their jobs. They were happy to do their part. Children in black neighborhoods chased after the empty buses. "No riders today!" they cried.

Never before had the black community of
Montgomery united in protest. And the bus
companies saw how much their business
depended on black riders.

The boycott was a huge success.

The boycott went on for more than a year.

Blacks in Montgomery walked to school and to work.

They walked to church. The leaders of the boycott organized private cars and vans to help out. Cabs took people for only ten cents, the same price as the bus fare. All over the country, people sent money to show their support. It helped to pay for gas and other expenses.

Many whites were angry. Blacks were fired from their jobs. Rosa was among them. The owner of the barbershop where Raymond worked part-time said he would fire anyone who talked about the boycott. Raymond quit in protest. Now Rosa had to take on sewing jobs so that they could get by. Still, the black community stayed united and strong.

On December 5, 1955, Rosa's trial began. Jim Blake, the bus driver, was the lead witness. Two white women on the bus that day were also witnesses. They lied, saying that there had been an empty seat in the back that Rosa had refused to take.

Rosa did not present her side of the story to the judges. Her lawyer did not want her to. In fact, he wanted her to be found guilty. Why? Because then her case would go to a higher court. Only a higher court had the power to end the bus rules.

The lawyer got his wish. Within a few minutes, Rosa was found guilty and fined fourteen dollars.

Was this the end? No. It was the beginning. Rosa's lawyer appealed the verdict. That means he

didn't think the verdict was fair. Judges in a higher court would get to hear Rosa's side of the case. Raymond had been right to fear for Rosa. She started to receive death threats over the phone.

Other civil rights leaders were threatened, too. Reverend King's house was bombed because he had spoken out in favor of the boycott.

Now that she was out of work, Rosa was able to devote more time and energy to the boycott. She began speaking about her experiences at churches and NAACP meetings. Her speeches raised money to help the bus boycott continue. She even flew to New York City to speak at Madison Square Garden. In New York, she met Eleanor Roosevelt, the wife of former president Franklin Roosevelt. Eleanor Roosevelt was a longtime champion of civil rights.

ELEANOR ROOSEVELT

ELEANOR ROOSEVELT WAS MARRIED TO FRANKLIN ROOSEVELT, PRESIDENT FROM 1933 TO 1945. SHE WAS A BIG SUPPORTER OF CIVIL RIGHTS. IN 1938, WHILE ATTENDING A CONFERENCE IN BIRMINGHAM, ALABAMA, SHE DID NOT WANT TO SIT IN THE ALL-WHITE SECTION OF THE AUDITORIUM. SHE WANTED TO SIT WITH BLACK FRIENDS. SO SHE GOT UP AND MOVED TO THE BLACK SECTION ACROSS THE AISLE. A POLICE OFFICER TOLD HER THAT SHE WAS BREAKING THE LAW, SO SHE HAD A CHAIR PLACED IN THE CENTER OF THE AISLE AND SAT THERE INSTEAD. THE FOLLOWING YEAR, SHE PUBLICLY WITHDREW FROM THE DAUGHTERS OF THE AMERICAN REVOLUTION AFTER THE GROUP REFUSED TO LET BLACK SINGER MARIAN ANDERSON SING IN ITS AUDITORIUM.

Finally, everyone's hard work paid off. On
November 13, 1956, the United States Supreme
Court, the very highest court in the country,
said that bus segregation was unconstitutional.
Dr. Martin Luther King, Jr., said it was "a victory

for all mankind." He added, "At bottom, the universe is on the side of justice."

In December 1956, the black community of Montgomery was ready to get back on the bus. But this time, they did not have to ride in the back. Along with a reporter and photographer from *Look* magazine, Rosa got on the Cleveland Avenue bus. Jim Blake, the same bus driver who

had her arrested, was at the wheel. Rosa ignored him. She sat in one of the front seats and the reporter snapped her picture. The photograph is the most famous picture ever taken of her.

Rosa Parks was now a heroine.

Chapter 9
Moving Ahead

Yes, Rosa was a heroine. Her simple act of protest—refusing to give up a bus seat—is often seen as the beginning of the powerful civil rights movement of the 1960s. However, hard times were not over. Rosa received more hate mail and threatening phone calls. Raymond began to sleep with a loaded gun nearby. No one wanted to hire

her. How could she and her family get by? They would have to leave Montgomery.

Rosa, Raymond, and her mother moved to Detroit, where Rosa's brother, Sylvester, still lived. They settled into an apartment on the West Side of Detroit. Raymond attended barbershop school

 to get his Michigan license. Rosa found a job downtown, at the Stockton Sewing Company. She made aprons and skirts. It was a quiet job and she liked

it very much. She became involved with a local church and continued working for civil rights.

In August 1963, Rosa attended a historic civil rights march in Washington, D.C. Dr. King gave his famous "I Have a Dream" speech in front of the Lincoln Memorial. Rosa was thrilled by the number of people at the march. More than two hundred thousand people, white and black, attended. Although actress Josephine Baker spoke, Rosa was disappointed that women did

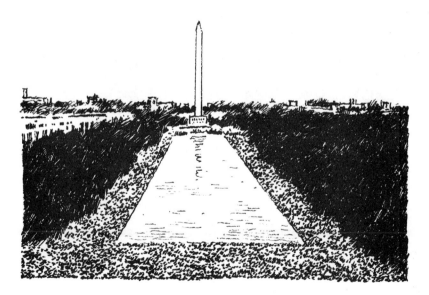

not have a bigger role at the event. Still, important changes were happening.

President Lyndon Johnson signed the Civil Rights Act in 1964. It was now a law that, among other things, black people had to be treated equally

at work or if they tried to buy a home. The
Voting Rights Act followed in 1965. It did away
with all the unfair rules that kept blacks from
voting. This was the cause that Rosa had fought
so hard for.

THE CIVIL RIGHTS ACT OF 1964

THE CIVIL RIGHTS ACT OF 1964, SIGNED BY PRESIDENT JOHNSON, WAS A GREAT MILESTONE IN GRANTING EQUAL RIGHTS TO MINORITIES. IT DID AWAY WITH THE JIM CROW LAWS THAT HAD ENFORCED SEGREGATION IN THE SOUTH FOR SO LONG. NOW ALL PEOPLE HAD THE RIGHT TO BE SERVED IN PUBLIC FACILITIES SUCH AS RESTAURANTS, THEATERS, LIBRARIES, AND HOTELS. A PUBLIC PLACE COULD NOT REMAIN "FOR WHITES ONLY." IF SCHOOLS DID NOT LET IN BLACK STUDENTS, THE SCHOOLS WOULD BE TAKEN TO COURT. COMPANIES WITH MORE THAN FIFTEEN EMPLOYEES HAD TO TREAT ALL WORKERS EQUALLY.

THEN, IN 1965, CAME THE EQUALLY IMPORTANT NATIONAL VOTING RIGHTS ACT. THIS MADE IT ILLEGAL FOR ANY STATE TO PREVENT SOMEONE FROM VOTING ON THE BASIS OF RACE OR COLOR. CONGRESS NOW OUTLAWED THE PRACTICE OF REQUIRING CITIZENS TO PASS UNFAIR READING OR LITERACY TESTS IN ORDER TO REGISTER TO VOTE.

With more blacks voting, black candidates began to enter politics. In 1964, John Conyers, Jr., who was from Detroit, ran for a seat in the US House of Representatives. Rosa was active in his campaign. And when he won, she went to work for him full-time. She answered his mail, organized

JOHN CONYERS, JR.

voter registration, and found jobs and homes for those who needed them. She did a lot of the same kind of work she did for the NAACP. But now she was paid for her efforts.

By the mid 1960s, Dr. Martin Luther King, Jr., was the most famous civil rights leader in the United States. Rosa greatly admired King. But she had trouble agreeing all the time with his message of nonviolence. King did not believe in ever fighting back. When a white man punched King in the face during a speech, King did not hit him. He wanted to offer love in place of hate. "I couldn't reach that point in my mind," Rosa once said. She was impressed by the words of another famous black leader, Malcolm X. Malcolm X encouraged blacks to be strong and to stand up for themselves. Sometimes that meant fighting for themselves.

The civil rights movement grew stronger throughout the 1960s. But with growth and strength came sorrow and pain. Black churches were bombed. In 1965, Malcolm X was killed. In 1968, Martin Luther King, Jr., was shot and killed. Rosa grieved for them all.

In 1975, Rosa returned to Montgomery for the twentieth anniversary of the bus boycott. Things had changed. Alabama had fifteen black lawmakers in the state government.

MALCOLM X

MALCOLM X WAS BORN MALCOLM LITTLE ON
MAY 19, 1925, IN OMAHA, NEBRASKA. MUCH OF HIS
CHILDHOOD WAS SPENT IN FOSTER HOMES AND
ORPHANAGES. MALCOLM GREW UP TO BECOME
A PETTY CRIMINAL AND WAS SENT TO PRISON.
THERE, HE BECAME A MUSLIM. HE DECIDED "LITTLE"
WAS A SLAVE NAME, AND TOOK THE NAME "X"
INSTEAD. "X" WAS MEANT TO SYMBOLIZE HIS LOST
AFRICAN TRIBAL NAME. WHEN HE GOT OUT
OF PRISON, HE WAS MADE A MINISTER. PEOPLE
ADMIRED HIM, AND HIS POPULARITY IN THE BLACK
COMMUNITY GREW. AT FIRST, MALCOLM X DID NOT
WISH TO IMPROVE RELATIONS BETWEEN THE
RACES. HE BELIEVED BLACKS SHOULD BUILD THEIR
OWN COMMUNITIES, APART FROM WHITES. BUT IN
1964, HE MADE A TRIP TO THE HOLY CITY OF
MECCA IN SAUDI ARABIA. THERE, HE SAID THAT HE
MET "BLONDE-HAIRED, BLUED-EYED MEN [HE]
COULD CALL [HIS] BROTHERS." WHEN HE RETURNED
TO THE UNITED STATES, HE SPOKE OF ALL RACES
LIVING TOGETHER. IN 1965, WHILE GIVING A SPEECH
IN NEW YORK CITY, MALCOLM X WAS SHOT TO
DEATH.

Since 1968, a black woman
from Brooklyn, New York,
had been a member of the US
Congress. Her name was Shirley
Chisholm. Many cities had
black mayors. Black studies
were offered at many colleges.
The works of black artists

SHIRLEY CHISHOLM

and writers gained new support and interest. This
progress made Rosa proud and happy.

Her private life was not so happy. Raymond
died of cancer in 1977. Three months later, Rosa's
brother died of the same disease. Her mother was
old and frail and had to move to a nursing home.

Rosa was alone now. She still had her job with John Conyers, Jr., and her church. And in 1987, she cofounded the Rosa and Raymond Parks Institute for Self Development in Detroit. It offered programs to help young people continue their education. Rosa had always felt a special bond with the young.

As she got older, Rosa Parks's achievements were more widely recognized. In 1979, she was given the Spingarn Medal by the NAACP. In 1996, President Bill Clinton awarded her the Presidential Medal of Freedom. She received the Congressional Gold Medal in 1999. The same  year, *TIME* magazine called her one of the twenty most important people of the twentieth century. She received awards, medals, and honorary degrees from all over the world. In 2000, the Rosa Parks Library and Museum opened in Montgomery.

Rosa had retired in 1988, at the age of seventy-five. Now she had more time. With the

help of a writer named Jim Haskins, she wrote a book about her life. It was called *Rosa Parks: My Story* and was published in 1992. She also wrote *Dear Mrs. Parks: A Dialogue with Today's Youth*, a collection of letters to her from children and her answers to them. Another book she wrote, *Quiet Strength*, came out in 1994.

On October 24, 2005, Rosa died at the age of
ninety-two. Before her funeral, her coffin was
brought to the Capitol building in Washington, D.C.,

so people could come and pay their respects to
Rosa Parks. It was the first time a woman had
been honored in that way. More than four

thousand people attended her funeral. She was buried in a cemetery in her adopted city of Detroit.

The woman who had refused to give up her seat helped change the world with her quiet courage. Some people thought Rosa did not get up because she was tired or because she was old. Rosa said no. Those were not the reasons. "I was not tired physically," she said, "or no more tired than I usually was at the end of a working day. I was not old, although some people have an image of me as being old then. I was forty-two. No, the only tired I was, was tired of giving in."

TIMELINE OF
ROSA PARKS'S LIFE

1913	Rosa Louise McCauley born in Tuskegee, Alabama
1924	Enrolls in Montgomery Industrial School for Girls
1932	Marries Raymond Parks
1934	Receives high school diploma
1943	Becomes secretary of the Montgomery chapter of the NAAC[
1944	Works at Maxwell Air Force Base
1945	Registers to vote
1955	Is arrested for refusing to give her bus seat to a white man on December 1; Montgomery Bus Boycott starts
1956	Montgomery Bus Boycott ends
1957	Moves to Detroit, Michigan
1965	Begins working for Rep. John Conyers, Jr., of Michigan
1977	Raymond Parks dies
1987	Establishes the Rosa and Raymond Parks Institute for Self Development
1988	Retires after more than twenty years in Conyers's office
1992	Publishes her first book, *Rosa Parks: My Story*, with Jim Haskins
1996	Receives highest US civilian honor, the Presidential Medal of Freedom
1999	Awarded the Congressional Gold Medal of Honor; Named by *TIME* magazine as one of the twenty most powerful and influential figures of the century
2005	Dies at 92

TIMELINE OF THE WORLD

Harriet Tubman dies	1913
World War I is fought in Europe	1914–1918
Women win the right to vote; Ku Klux Klan launches a recruitment campaign and gains 85,000 new recruits	1920
Great Depression begins in United States	1929
Franklin Roosevelt elected president for the first of four terms	1932
World War II begins in Europe	1939
Japanese bomb Pearl Harbor; United States enters World War II	1941
Ballpoint pens go on sale; World War II ends	1945
Jackie Robinson becomes first black baseball player for the Brooklyn Dodgers	1947
US Supreme Court rules that segregation in public schools is unconstitutional	1954
President John F. Kennedy assassinated in Dallas, Texas	1963
Beatlemania hits the United States	1964
Malcolm X assassinated in New York City	1965
Dr. Martin Luther King, Jr., assassinated	1968
Sesame Street first airs on television	1969
E-mail invented by Ray Tomlinson	1972
Sandra Day O'Connor becomes first woman on the US Supreme Court	1981
September 11th attacks occur in United States	2001

BIBLIOGRAPHY

*Ashby, Ruth. **Rosa Parks: Courageous Citizen.** Sterling, New York, 2008.

*Bjornlund, Lydia. **Rosa Parks and the Montgomery Bus Boycott.** Lucent Books, Detroit, 2008.

Brinkley, Douglas. **Rosa Parks: A Penguin Life.** Penguin Group (USA), New York, 2000.

*Davis, Kenneth C. **Don't Know Much About Rosa Parks.** HarperCollins, New York, 2005.

*Parks, Rosa, with Jim Haskins. **Rosa Parks: My Story.** Penguin Group (USA), New York, 1992.

*Starred books are for young readers.

8